The Woke Salaryman
Crash Course on Capitalism & Money

Goh Wei Choon
He Ruiming

WILEY

Registered Office(s)
John Wiley & Sons, Inc., 111 River Street, Hoboken, NJ 07030, USA
John Wiley & Sons Singapore Pte. Ltd, 134 Jurong Gateway Road, #04-307H, Singapore 600134

For details of our global editorial offices, customer services, and more information about Wiley products visit us at www.wiley.com.

Library of Congress Cataloging-in-Publication Data Is Available:

ISBN 9781394226528 (Paperback)
ISBN 9781394226542 (ePDF)
ISBN 9781394226535 (ePub)

Cover Design and Illustration: The Woke Salaryman

Set in 12/14.4 The Woke Salaryman 2023-Regular by Straive, India

SKY10065011_011324

CONTENTS

PREFACE

Dear reader,

If I had to guess about you, I would think:

You're a young person born into a developed country. Life is supposed to be good, but it doesn't feel like it.

Inequality is rising. Job opportunities are few. Those with family connections have advantages you can only dream of. You have a degree from a university, but it doesn't seem to be helping you much. Rich and supposedly skilled foreigners are coming into your city, your country.

They're driving prices up. Rent is skyrocketing. Cars are expensive. You can barely afford housing in the places you were born.

Amidst all of this, your government seems to be sitting on their hands, doing nothing.

They're giving the rich tax breaks instead of taxing them. Giving them things, instead of distributing wealth.

At the same time, YOU'RE saddled with debt. Lots of it. It almost feels like they're not on your side at all.

And for that reason, you probably hate capitalism. Why would it be any different?

It's an inherently unfair system, where those born with more resources are given a massive head start in life.

Is there anything we can do about this inherently unfair, unjust system?

Well, there absolutely is. You can lobby governments for change. You can boycott companies. You might even want to start a revolution.

But here's the thing: change is a costly and long-drawn process.

To change this inherently unfair system, you have to first amass power in the form of resources. Organize labour. Get your own freedom.

It's most likely that you will have to get rich first.

And this is what this book is about. Amassing power and wealth to change the world for good.

Instead of villainizing or glorifying capitalism, we have a different proposal for you. Study the rules of wealth and capitalism, free of moral judgement.

Learn as if you were mastering math; you don't have to love it, but you have to accept that it exists and play by the rules.

We wish you all the best.

The Woke Salaryman
He Ruiming & Goh Wei Choon

ACCEPT THAT LIFE IS UNFAIR

Equality is an aspiration.
It is not reality;
it is not practical.

\- Lee Kuan Yew
founding Prime Minister of Singapore

ACCEPT THAT LIFE IS UNFAIR

During my first week at a French multinational advertising agency in 2014, a senior colleague shared something with me that left a lasting impact.

'In the advertising industry in Singapore, and even across Asia, race matters. There's no easy way to say it. It's easier for white people to succeed. They are seen as more creative. If you're from the UK, the US, or even Australia, your chances of becoming a creative director are higher. You're a local Chinese Singaporean, 'they told me,' so you're not exactly high up the colour bar.'

A mix of shame and rage coursed through me.

I believed I deserved an equal chance to rise through the ranks, regardless of my background or nationality.

Yet, I couldn't deny the reality of the situation. I had witnessed how local clients treated expat creative directors with more respect.

The higher up the management ladder, the fewer locals there were, and the more European names prevailed.

How should anyone react in this situation? When faced with unfairness and injustice, I believe there are <u>two</u> valid approaches to consider:

<u>The first is to strive for structural change</u>

I could advocate for equal opportunities for locals or urge the government to investigate the issue. Perhaps they could implement a quota system that ensures a certain number of locals become creative directors each year.

However, let's be honest, there are limitations to what can be done. The evidence of preferential treatment for expats in this industry is mostly anecdotal. What if there are valid reasons, albeit intangible, that clients prefer European faces for their accounts?

<u>The second approach is to focus on what we CAN control</u>

While I couldn't immediately change the industry's perception and prove that locals are equally capable of producing creative work, I could work on improving myself. I could demonstrate that I was hardworking, intelligent, and, yes, creative. For instance, by addressing stereotypes that Asian individuals are shy and unassertive, I could develop my skills as a presenter and speaker.

I could also choose to leave companies where expats enjoyed unfair advantages and seek opportunities where fairness prevailed. In fact, I could even save up and start my own company to directly compete.

Personally, I have chosen to channel my energy into the <u>second</u> approach rather than the first. To do this, I've had to accept that life is unfair.

It doesn't take a genius to realize that we have no control over the circumstances we are born into.

A person born in a developed nation has far more options than someone born into a less developed one. Genetics also play a role; unequal treatment based on ethnicity is prevalent in many parts of the world. Even in matters of romance, people often exhibit preferences for qualities such as wealth, height, size, or complexion.

Also, the era we are born into significantly influences our quality of life. A Chinese person born today will undoubtedly enjoy better living conditions than someone born during, say, the Cultural Revolution of the 1950s.

Interestingly, this concept extends to nations as well. Some countries are blessed with abundant natural resources, while others grapple with historical disadvantages.

Colonization, for instance, elevated Europe to become one of the wealthiest continents and left Africa struggling as one of the poorest.

Does it hurt to lack the advantages that others have?

Absolutely.

We empathize with the feelings of hopelessness and defeat that arise from such disparities. These emotions are valid, natural, and should be acknowledged.

However, let's also recognize the true cost of harbouring resentment. It takes real energy to remain angry, and it hinders our personal growth, friendships, and skill development. Thinking 'Why bother trying if the world is unfair and others have it better?' can be paralyzing.

There's a favourite quote of ours regarding resentment:

> Resentment is like taking poison and waiting for the other person to die.

Coming to terms with the unfairness of the world is a painful and protracted process, but it is also liberating.

Understandably, it takes time. We would expect most individuals to move past the initial resentment by their 30s, but there are many who struggle to let go even well into their 40s, 50s, or 60s.

To those individuals, we say this: your feelings are valid, and they deserve acknowledgement. No one has the right to demand that you 'get over it.'

Take the time to reflect on the injustices of the world. Allow yourself to be angry and rage against the system. Vent your frustrations thoroughly.

Then, when you're ready, find closure.

<u>Only then</u> can you begin to change your life for the better.

The following chapter will explore aspects within your control and those that are not. We hope these insights will assist you in navigating the inherently unjust world we live in.

How much in life is actually up to you?

ORIGINALLY PUBLISHED:
12 APR 2022

〜〜〜〜〜〜〜

Before you embark on your financial journey, it's important to realize that a great many people are poor due to no fault of their own.

The following comic describes the vicious cycle of poverty.

In sociology, there's a concept called:

STRUCTURE VS Agency

These two factors make HUGE impacts on how our lives play out.

STRUCTURE:

Stuff that influences or limits
choices and opportunities available.

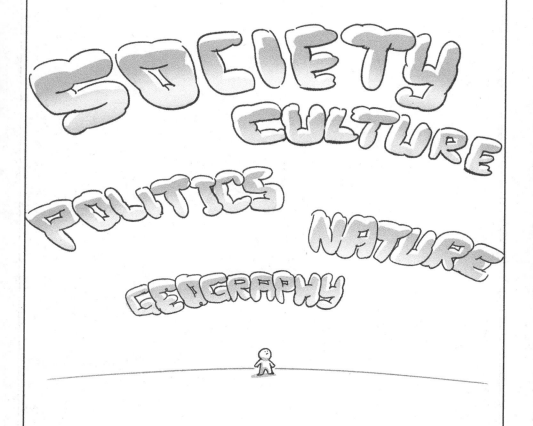

As a personal finance page focused on self-improvement, we often focus a lot on agency – what the person can do.

These include:

- Your habits
- The company you keep

- Your values
- Your ability to make the right decisions

In this analogy agency means the parts on your ship which you can modify and optimize.

NETWORK

INVEST

EARNING POWER

SAVINGS

Structure can be where you're born:

If you are born into a developed country, it's far easier to invest than if you were born into an undeveloped country.

Structure can be classist:

If you are born into a less well-off family, you might find it harder to make important connections that might help in your career.

What does this mean?

The obvious implication is that life is definitely unfair, and we start off at unequal points with unequal resources.

For that reason, it's important to be empathetic to others less privileged, and be grateful for the opportunities you have.

Remember, people don't choose whether they start off rich or poor.

On another level it also means that everyone has not only different **paths** to success, but different **definitions** of success.

For someone who inherited wealth, success could be creating a multibillion dollar company.

Finally, there is no such thing as being in 100% control of your destiny.

But it's important to acknowledge that you have a role to play in your own life.

After all, you may not be able to write your destiny 100%.

But you may be able to shift the course with your actions.

We cannot direct the wind and the oceans, but we can adjust the sails.

The Four Horsemen of Success

ORIGINALLY PUBLISHED:
08 DEC 2022

~~~~~~

Hard work is potent, but it's a poor predictor of success on its own.

Here are some other factors that we think are often overlooked in the general perception of what it takes to attain success.

THE FOUR HORSEMEN OF SUCCESS YOU'LL JUST NEED TO ACCEPT

We often attribute success to hard work. And sometimes, this can lead to notions of someone who is not successful just because they are lazy.

That couldn't be further from the truth. Why? Because hard work alone doesn't guarantee success. No one should ever think that.

Here's an example:

Digging a hole for two weeks non-stop is an impressive display of hard work. But the effort probably won't produce a very deep hole. Especially compared to someone who has the advantage of say, a shovel.

I think it is important to recognize that other factors are involved in being successful. Here are the four biggest ones we think have the most impact:

PRIVILEGE

There have been a lot of great conversations about privilege lately. Privilege is the kind of the advantage you're born with.

PRIVILEGE

POTENTIAL: ⭐⭐⭐⭐◉   IMPACT: ⭐⭐◉◉◉

INHERITANCE:
Flip 5 coins at the start of the game. For every head, get $100k in start-up capital.

GREAT EXPECTATIONS:
+20 STRESS if player is not in the lead.

If you're born into a rich family, you have the privilege of a safety net to take risks. Of course, this is not just limited to wealth.

If you aren't a minority - whether due to your race, sexual orientation, or physical or mental ability - you have privilege because chances are, you will face less discrimination.

In addition, beyond these two popular narratives about privilege, perhaps it's worth thinking of the other forms of privilege; these can involve the era or place where you are born.

We have the privilege of being born in modern-day Singapore - currently a relatively safe country where the life expectancy is high, and infant mortality is low.

You generally have no control over what privilege you receive, nor should you be ashamed of having it.

What is important is that you realize that it has some role to play in your success. The more privilege you have, the easier it is for you to find success. No one should ever deny that.

That will help you be more empathetic, as opposed to saying, 'Oh, the poor are just lazy.'

That said, it's also important to point out that while it is many things, privilege is not everything.

Think about it: if privilege were everything, then Jeff Bezos wouldn't be the richest person in the world today - after all, Bezos' dad started off as a broke immigrant when he arrived in America, speaking only Spanish.

Perhaps what is more accurate to say is that if you reach a certain level of privilege, you stand a good chance of achieving financial success.

Which brings us to...

EFFORT

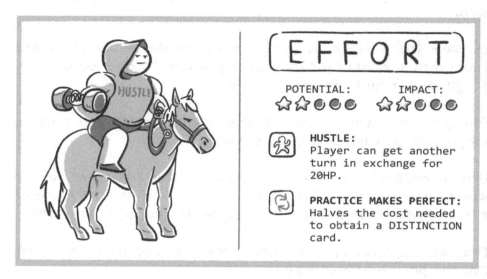

EFFORT

POTENTIAL: ☆☆●●● IMPACT: ☆☆●●●

HUSTLE:
Player can get another turn in exchange for 20HP.

PRACTICE MAKES PERFECT:
Halves the cost needed to obtain a DISTINCTION card.

Generally, 'effort' or 'hard work' are the default factors people always fall back on when they have to explain their success. You might say this is purposefully disingenuous; but consider this explanation:

Telling someone 'I was born rich' or 'I was lucky' does not make for good interview material.

On the other hand, 'I did xxx things differently' and elaborating on how might give away any competitive advantage you have.

'I put in a lot of effort' then becomes the most convenient answer to give. Not to mention it's often semi-true: working hard is often a prerequisite for success, even for people from privileged backgrounds.

Because of its disproportionate role in making sense of success, effort is the most inspirational of all the horsemen. It's also the most relatable, and it makes for good storytelling, because everyone can put in hard work.

Still, that doesn't change the fact that effort and hard work matter and they're massive game-changers. Passion and perseverance for long-term goals are often more important than things like IQ.

Make no mistake: practice still makes perfect, and there is no substitute for hard work. It's just that there are more factors at play you need to consider.

DISTINCTION

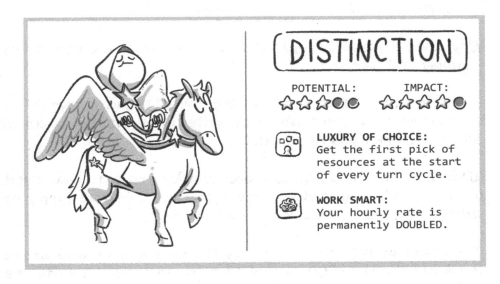

The next factor is something I struggled to name, but I'm going to call it distinction - or the ability to do something different from others. Being unconventional, or innovative.

Distinction, or the lack of it, is probably why many of us can spend 12 hours a day working, yet receive no benefits from it.

Here's the concept in action applied to freelance writing:

As a freelance writer, I get paid anywhere from $50 - $2,000 for an article.

What I've learnt is that the $50 articles are generally stuff that almost anyone who can string a sentence can write.

For example:
<Five things to do in Singapore when you're bored>.

Why does it pay only $50? It boils down to simple economics - supply and demand.

I try not to take on projects like these, because there's an oversupply of writers who can write <Five things to do in Singapore when you're bored>.

What I rather focus on is more complex projects that need more specialist knowledge - where there is a limited supply of writers, and yes, they'll pay more than $50.

The result at the end of the day is that someone who writes ten $50 articles ($500) would earn the same as if I write one $500 article about the pros-and-cons of term versus whole life insurance.

Yes, they worked harder, but we would have earned the same amount of money.

The lesson here is this: skills and knowledge matter. So do out-of-the-box thinking, creativity, and resourcefulness.

If you work like everyone and think like everyone, then don't expect to achieve extraordinary levels of success.

LUCK

Luck is the wildcard and also the most painful one we have to grapple with because, much like privilege, this is something we have no direct control over.

Extreme example:

You can save 100k before 30, buy all the health insurance you need, build various sources of passive forms of income; but still have your life destroyed by a catastrophic car accident (unlikely but possible).

Less extreme example:

You can upskill yourself, create the perfect resume, network, have the best ideas... but sometimes success just doesn't come. And the sad reality is that we have to accept this.

But lest you think we have no way of mitigating luck, I think it's useful to think of it as throwing dice.

You cannot control if you roll a six on a dice each time.

But, you can increase the odds of getting a six if you...

- Keep throwing until you get a six (Effort)

- Master the art of throwing dice (Distinction)

- Have many sets of dice given to you at birth (Privilege)

The game of cards you now must play

Life is like a game of cards. Some of us get blessed with privilege. Others are cursed with bad luck. Without judgement, this is an unfair system we are born into.

It is important to acknowledge it.

It is also important to understand it.

But ultimately, if you want to succeed, understanding the rules is important. Without it, you might put in lots of effort for very little in return, which is a surefire way to disillusionment.

That said, now you know the cards. It's time for you to play the game.*

Stay woke, salaryman.

*If you so wish to. This article defines success in conventional terms which is linked to material wealth. Your own definition of success might be different and that is okay, there is no judgement on our part.

Stop blaming the poor for being poor

ORIGINALLY PUBLISHED:
24 OCT 2022

~~~~~~

As you embark on your financial journey, you will start to become more aware of everyone's financial backgrounds. It's easy to glorify the rich and villainize the poor, but it's important to realize that a great many people are poor, due to no fault of their own.

Stop blaming the poor for being poor

But for the people who don't have a
lot of income, this is more complicated.

Lots of financial tips are not applicable
if you have a low income.

For example, saving **20%** your income
when you earn $6000 is <u>easy</u>.

Saving when you earn $600 is <u>not</u>.

One of these effects is stress. It can be hard to make good decisions when you are under a lot of stress.

This stress can lead to family violence, unhealthy addictions, and poor health. All of which are very costly.

Also, impoverished people can sometimes end up <u>spending more</u> than average.

For example, they may have no choice but to buy cheaper products that spoil faster, spending more in the long run.

Lower-income folks also may end up paying more in terms of time.

For example, they may not have many options when it comes to commuting, so they end up walking a lot, or taking public transport when a cab would be more efficient.

Lower-income folks sometimes also pay in health. For example, they may not be able to afford proper mattresses, and thus cannot get proper rest.

This impacts their ability to then perform well at work, thus reducing their ability to break out of the poverty cycle.

Bad decisions compound over time, and can make climbing out of poverty exponentially more difficult - or even impossible without external help.

The final outcome we should be striving for is impact. Instead:

① Withhold blame and judgement.

② Practice empathy.

③ Take concrete action and make an impact.

START YOUR FINANCIAL REVOLUTION

The principles of building
wealth are simple.

But simple doesn't mean easy.

- Us

CHAPTER 2
START YOUR
FINANCIAL REVOLUTION

The start of your financial journey is usually confusing. Like many young adults, I found myself bombarded with differing pieces of advice.

Most financial gurus say that to be wealthy, you need to start investing or trading as early as possible. Others say it's about cutting down expenses and living below your means. Still, others say that it's about becoming an entrepreneur and escaping the 9-5 grind.

Each of these pieces of advice has its merits but, taken to extremes, can be more harmful than helpful. Here's how we'd like to think of it.

There are four activities when it comes to growing wealth. The more of them you can do successfully, the higher your chances.

These are:

Earning

We think this is the most important of them all, especially in the early stages of your financial journey. If you don't earn, you cannot save. If you cannot save, you cannot invest. Neither will you have any wealth to protect.

Your earning ability largely depends on your skills, your network, and your ability to take risks. But a whole bunch of other things matter too.

Saving and spending

Your ability to save is your ability to retain wealth. If you're bad at saving money, expect wealth to simply come and go. Without the discipline to save wealth, you'll be building castles in the sand.

Many people will be surprised to know that many high-income earners are terrible at saving. A banker earning $20,000 might have less savings than someone in a regular office job. The world is just strange that way.

Investing

In recent times, investing (and trading, its shorter-term cousin) has been portrayed as the magic bullet for financial independence. This is somewhat true, but it doesn't show us the full picture.

Yes, investing is crucial in allowing you to grow your wealth while you're not working. Over time, the gulf between those who invest, and those who don't is immense.

BUT, investing also comes with risk. Often in the pursuit of fast and high returns, people lose money instead of making it.

Done poorly, investments are often counterproductive.

Protecting

Even the best-laid financial plans can go awry. Getting into an accident or falling sick, can potentially be expensive. That's where stuff like insurance and risk management comes in.

Now, going into the intricacies of earning, saving, investing and protecting would require an entire book in itself.

For the sake of brevity, we've chosen to focus on what we think will be most useful to a young adult.

The first $100k is the hardest, but it gets easier

ORIGINALLY PUBLISHED:
22 MAR 2022

~~~~~~~

The journey to your first $100,000 is not going to be an easy one, but here's why it's worth the trouble (and why it gets easier).

Reason 1: The power of habit

Now, I spend just slightly more compared to my 25-year-old self, despite earning more.

The habits I developed on the way to my first $100k kept me very safe from lifestyle inflation.

The first $100,000 is growth.

The next $100,000 is maintenance.

The lack of skills, experience, and network meant rejections and failures.

But eventually, the hard work paid off.

The skills, experience, and network you gain along the way don't just magically disappear.

You'll start the journey to your next $100k with these resources already in place.

Imagine you invested your first $100,000 in the stock market, and it gave you $5,000 in returns.
RETURNS
Thank you.
Enjoy!

Here's something people often forget about wealth.

Having more of it allows you to take more risk, and hence gain greater rewards.

On the extreme end,
if you were a millionaire, you'll be
able to put 90% of your wealth in
high-risk, high-reward assets.

You'd have a full
$100,000 in
emergency funds.
Not bad at all.

If you're starting out from zero as a 25-year-old, I completely understand how daunting and hopeless it must feel.

Don't let anyone tell you saving a six-figure amount is easy.

Because it isn't.

I'll never get up there!

You can do it!

Young people are obsessed with investing. Here's why they should not be

ORIGINALLY PUBLISHED:
21 OCT 2022

~~~~~~

A lot of youth are convinced that they will build wealth through investing.

We think it's misplaced; and the smartest thing most young people can do is bet on themselves.

A long time ago, here's how I thought I would make my first $100,000.

I would take several years to save $10,000. Then I would make an extremely good investment.

This did not happen.

I did save my $10,000. But when I tried to invest it and turn it into $100,000, I was sorely disappointed.

After an entire year in the stock market, it only grew by $1,200.

REALITY

This was 12%. A far cry from 10x (which was 1000%).

Warren Buffett, the world's most famous investor, managed only 20% per annum from 1965-2021.

Industry professionals will be considered 'decent' if they manage more than 10% over the long term.

For the average person, who doesn't invest full time, 5-8% is a more realistic number.

* But remember that all investments have risks! You won't be making money every year. You could also lose all your money.

FAMOUS INVESTOR   20%

INDUSTRY PROFESSIONALS   10%

AVERAGE PERSON   5-8%

Investing won't earn you a lot at the start

Let's use $10k as an example.

Huh.

(This is how much you'll earn based on a very realistic 7% return per year.)

When your capital is small,
your returns are also small.

Most of us don't start off with
$1,000,000 in life, so at this stage,
your efforts are best served
by increasing your **capital.**

How to increase your capital?
Work on your earning power.

Instead of focusing on picking stocks,
consider learning in-demand skills,
negotiating for an increment,
or doing a side hustle.

Negotiating salary
+
Starting a side hustle
+
Getting a better
paying job

$4K per year

$4K per year

$12K per year

VS

Investment returns

$700

Once you improve your income, you will have more capital, and your investment returns will increase as well.

And once you do this for long enough, your investments will indeed make you wealthy.

What should you do with this information?

**1) Forget about getting
rich quick via investing.**

This often leads to people taking too
much risk, leading to financial setbacks.

2) Invest early with realistic expectations.

Don't get us wrong. Investing is still important. Just remember it won't be the main driver of wealth from $0-$100,000 (or even $1,000,000)

But every bit counts!

3) Work on your earning power.

There is no substitute for having a good network and in-demand soft + hard skills.

Let's take a closer look at all three and how they interplay:

Hard Skills are technical skills often specific to your industry.

Some examples:

- Software proficiency and coding ability
- Foreign language skills
- SEO marketing
- And other professional certifications

Soft Skills are non-technical skills that will enhance (often greatly) what you can command.

Some examples:

- Communication
- Teamwork
- Problem-solving
- Time management
- Critical thinking
- Empathy

Finally, a **good network** will connect your **soft skills** and **hard skills** with people who are willing to pay for them.

Don't ignore this!

Remember, that YOU are the best investment you can make.

Stay woke, salaryman.

The 10 timeless principles to increase your income

ORIGINALLY PUBLISHED:
12 SEP 2022

~~~~~~~~

Your job often has a huge impact on how much you will earn.

Understanding and accepting the reasons why some jobs are paid more/less is crucial.

It also helps you make more informed decisions about what to expect from a job.

The 10 timeless principles to increase your income

By now, you've seen the memes. They go something like this:

To make a super comfortable income at 30, you need to:

- Have cold showers in the morning at 4 a.m
- Read about investments and asset classes
- Learn to manage upwards
- Have multimillionaire parents who own the company

We can relate and appreciate people taking pot-shots at extremely privileged folks pretending to be self-made.

That said, it's also important to acknowledge that not all high-income earners are spoilt kids running a family business.

Here's a humbling truth: there are indeed people earning way above the median salary of $4,680 in their 20s or 30s.

It is not unheard of for people to earn $10,000–$15,000 by the time they're 30.

With that said, here are some starting points for you to look at if you want to increase your income, no matter what role you're in (there is some overlap in some of them.)

1. Work more or work harder

The lowest-hanging fruit when it comes to increasing your take-home salary is to work longer hours. It is the most straightforward way. It is also our least favourite way.

In theory, it makes sense. If you earn $40 an hour, you'll earn more if you work 200 hours ($8,000), as opposed to 100 hours ($4,000) a month.

In the real world, this will not apply to many salaried employees who are remunerated on a monthly basis.

This is the first and most important lesson: Hard work alone is often not enough to increase your income. It certainly helps, but it hardly guarantees it.

Understanding this will allow you to put your efforts to better use elsewhere.

2. Switch to a more lucrative industry

Some industries will just earn more than others.

This is the uncomfortable truth: How much you are paid is a combination of

- Supply and demand
- Who's paying you
- What's your impact

What this means is that our career choices will directly affect our income. It is highly unlikely for an entry-level accountant to be paid $10,000 a month. But it is more likely for a junior software engineer.

This has nothing to do with whether people work hard or not. Or who is morally superior. Instead, it all boils down to how much people are willing to pay for your skills.

If you want to increase your income, there are indeed industries that will likely pay more (these are always changing, but current in-demand fields include information & communications and tech.)

That said, switching industries may mean giving up your passion, work-life balance, benefits, purpose, and culture, or investing time to learn a new skill. You may also the lack natural aptitude needed to do the job.

This is why we don't recommend jumping on the bandwagon of 'what's hot' with money as the ONLY consideration.

3. Cut out the middleman

When you work for a company, a boss earns a mark-up on your labour, aka profit margin.

For example, you earn $4,000, and your boss charges the client $10,000. They take $4,000.

Effectively, they are the middleman between you and the people willing to pay for your skills.

If you could do the middleman's job, you could be pocketing that extra $4,000.

That said, it would be disingenuous to pretend that middlemen don't provide any value. It takes money, time, skills, and networks needed to find business, as well as the labour needed to work on projects.

The simplest way to cut out the middleman? Try being a freelancer or becoming self-employed.

4. Take on risk and forgo stability

When you work at a company as an employee, you risk no capital. Whether or not the company makes money or not, you'll receive a paycheck every month. It's a stable life.

If you're a business owner, you take on quite a large amount of risk. If the company doesn't make money, you still need to pay rent, salaries, bills, and whatnot.

However, in a scenario where the company does make money, the business owner will get a larger share of the profits. The employee will still get their regular salary.

From this example, you'll see that taking on **more risk** can mean *potentially* **more money.**

One classic example: Many commission-based sales jobs can pay handsomely if you do well at them; the sky's the limit.

The downside? It will punish you for not having results.

5. Negotiate, negotiate, negotiate

Most people (including yourself) put their self-interests first. Same when it comes to salary.

You'll be trying to get the most salary. Your employer will be trying to pay you what they can afford. Some clients will try to pay you as little as possible.

Without negotiation, you're more likely to get a deal that leans towards favouring the other party.

How do you negotiate better? Here are some starting points

- Understanding what you can charge for your skills based on the market rate (go for interviews often just to get an assessment).
- Knowing how to be assertive, and fight for what you are worth.
- Leaving the conversation open for future negotiations.
- Building up the ability to walk away from bad deals.
- Recognize when you have negotiating power, and when you don't.

That being said, even the best negotiators are limited by whether they can back their talk up. This brings us to...

6. Become irreplaceable

Do work that others can't do. The lower the barrier of entry, the lower the salary. Jobs that require special knowledge, skill and/or talent will generally pay more.

This is why handing out leaflets pays less than flying a commercial airliner. Or why doing basic data entry works pays less than successfully structuring a legal merger and acquisition deal.

Do work that others are unwilling to do. If you have difficulty acquiring the above, then taking on conventionally unpleasant or riskier jobs is an alternative.

Example:

- F&B staff get paid more to work on Christmas or New Year's Eve.
- Many advertising agencies also charge a rush fee when clients need things delivered on short notice.
- In the military, there are things such as 'risk' or 'hazard' pay for people in more dangerous roles.

None of these things are pleasant. But they will help you earn more money.

7. Lead people and learn how to organize labour

Elon Musk allegedly said: 'You get paid in direct proportion to the difficulty of problems you solve.'

Well, the more people you handle – and are responsible for – the bigger the problems you can solve.

Of course, this requires you to hone your management and leadership skills – which don't always come naturally.

Because of this, there are plenty of people with the title of 'manager' who have little or no leadership ability, and stagnate at the lowest levels of corporate because of this. (Further reading: the Peter principle)

The topic of leadership is something that we can't cover in one paragraph, or even one article. However, we think developing the following skills/traits is a great starting point for anyone who wants to be a leader.

- Reliability
- Communication and empathy
- Big-picture thinking
- Self-awareness
- Persuasion

8. Write and speak well

If a tree falls in the forest - and there's no one else to hear it - does it make a sound?

Similarly, if you have a great idea or execution - and you can't express it - can you honestly expect people to read your mind?

In Singapore, where people tend to be shy and reserved when it comes to speaking out at the workplace, being the outspoken and confident one, can give you an unfair advantage. (See above: Do work that others can't do.)

Learning how to communicate your ideas and convince clients will instantly make you more valuable.

But don't take it from us: Warren Buffett himself says that doing this can increase your net worth by up to 50%.

Further reading: Why you need to market yourself.

9. Join profit centres

The vast majority of companies will try to bring costs down, and increase profits.

This means there are cost centres and profit centres.

Often, this is also reflected in how their staff are paid. Staff who contribute directly to a company's profits will have a higher chance of being paid more.

Classic examples of cost centres are: accounting, human resources, and maintenance.

Profit centres...are well, most obviously the sales department.

(Do note it's possible for a role to be a cost centre in one company and a profit centre in another.)

10. Know your worth and be ready to move

It is entirely possible for someone to be able to command $10,000 somewhere else but be paid $4,000 for a role.

This is particularly true if you undervalue yourself, or refuse to leave despite knowing this.

How might you come to such a situation? Here are some common observations:

- Low self-esteem (possibly due to gaslighting)
- Misplaced loyalty in a company
- Refusal to leave a comfortable environment due to the fear of the unknown (for example, due to too many financial responsibilities)
- In-demand skills, in an industry that cannot pay

Admittedly, not all of these are easily addressed, yet, the opportunity cost for these can be quite large in the long term.

Our thoughts? Take however long you need to resolve them.

If it's low self-esteem, surround yourself with people who believe in you.

If it's a lack of network, go out there and meet people.

If it's a money situation, slowly build up the ability to make a career jump.

Remember, you can change things. You can move. You can learn.

You are not a tree.

Stay woke, salaryman.

Why you should think like a business (sometimes)

ORIGINALLY PUBLISHED:
27 JAN 2023

~~~~~~~~~

People spend huge portions of their waking hours in jobs working for businesses.

Yet, many of us still cling to misplaced notions of corporate loyalty, which can be a major barrier to increasing our earning power.

Why you should think like a business (sometimes)

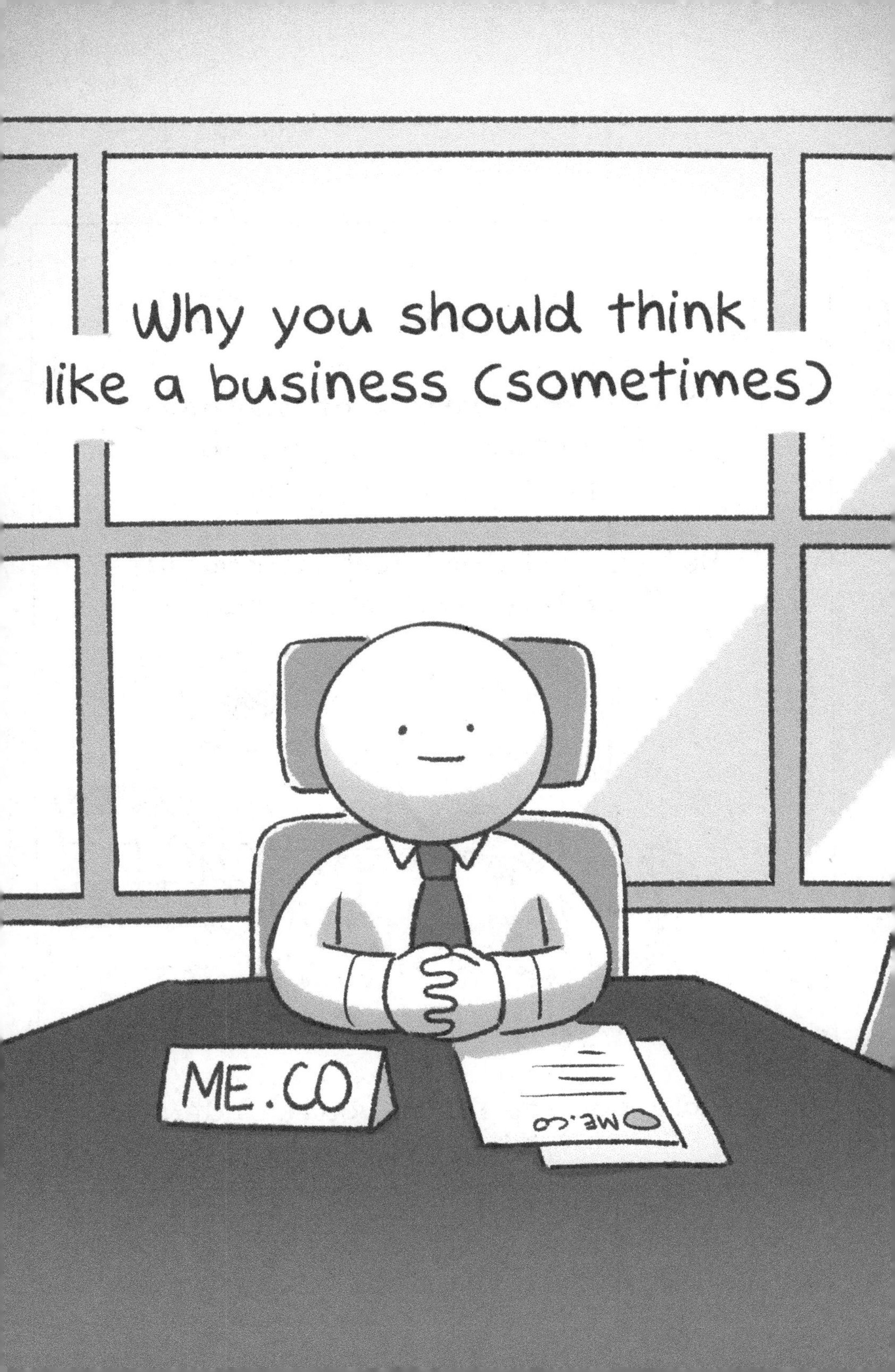

POV:

You've been working at company.
And you've given it your all
for the past 5 years.

But yet you don't feel appreciated.
You feel you're underpaid.

Actually, no. You KNOW you're underpaid.

Yet, you don't want to leave.

Why? Because you feel like you're abandoning the relationships you've built at work.

You feel like you're betraying the company.

Well, you might think of yourself as an employee working at a company.

But if you think about it, what you're actually doing is **selling your services** to the company on a monthly basis.

That makes you a service provider.
You're a business, selling services!

Your salary? That's the monthly subscription
fee your company pays to have you.

They do one of three things.

1. Get more business.

2. Increase prices.

3. End the relationship.

Let's examine.

Get more businesses

When businesses don't make money from one client, they will get more clients.

In your case, you might want to consider getting a side-hustle, or another job to supplement your income.

Of course, this is not always possible. This brings us to...

Increase prices

Businesses increase prices all the time.
They don't even ask permission.

They just increase prices and
see how their customers react.

If it's too high, they'll lower the prices.

End the partnership

Businesses end relationships when it no longer works for them. Happens all the time.

Similarly, it's okay to leave a job when it no longer makes sense for you.

It doesn't matter if your boss says they're not letting you quit.

It doesn't matter if people say you're letting your colleagues down.

When you have to go, you go.

Our take?

To deal with certain companies,
you must be able to think like a company.

THE REALITIES OF THE 2020s

Context is everything.

– Anon

CHAPTER 3
THE REALITIES OF THE 2020s

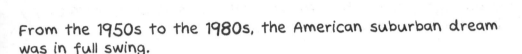

From the 1950s to the 1980s, the American suburban dream was in full swing.

The middle class could afford large homes with white picket fences, whilst raising two kids. Maybe a car or two. Wages were steadily rising and lives were improving year after year.

As future generations would find out the hard way, this dream would gradually become increasingly unattainable, except for a privileged few.

The wages for many jobs stagnated by the 1970s. Social mobility fell. The broad middle class eroded as income inequalities widened.

While the working class struggled, the wealthy few were able to give their children the opportunities to succeed, creating a vicious cycle of wealth concentration and even more inequality.

In Singapore, it was slightly different. Post-independence from 1965 to the early 2000s, we had our own boom. Because of our land scarcity, the middle class aspired for apartments instead of large homes.

In 1980, my parents bought their public housing for about $80,000 Singapore dollars. The nation's median salary was about $2,200.

Today, that same flat is worth over $600,000. That's more than 7 times what it was. The median salary is about $5,000. Just slightly more than double what it was. Wage growth simply has not kept up with property prices.

Today, in many advanced economies around the world, a similar pattern can be observed.

Young people in major cities — from New York and Taipei to Berlin, London, Melbourne, and Hong Kong — increasingly find it challenging to afford homes in the very neighbourhoods they grew up in, though the intensity of this challenge varies.

You might be tempted to ask: Where did we go wrong? But in reality, the question is more of 'what has changed.'

And changed it has.

Consider these shifts, for example.

People are living longer. Life expectancy has increased in the developed world, this means increased competition for housing, job opportunities, and resources. In Singapore, we've gone from 72 (1980) to 83 (2020).

Popular places are becoming MORE popular. Fewer people are living in rural areas, drawn to cities for better economic opportunities. This, in turn, means more competition within cities. In Singapore, we've grown from 2.4 million (1980) to 5.4 million (2020).

Globalization has also meant the mobility of talent, capital, and wealth across international borders, resulting in further competition within popular cities. About 43% of Singapore's population are immigrants. That's compared to 37% in London and San Franciso, and 29% in New York.

Technology has also significantly reshaped industries. Automation, digitalization, and artificial intelligence have transformed the nature of work, leading to job displacement in certain sectors.

Further education has lost its shine. Once a clear advantage in the job market in many developed economies, a college or university degree no longer guarantees the security it once did.

Without understanding these shifts and the causes behind them, it's easy to be filled with bitterness and resentment.

This is true, whether you're an elderly person chastising the younger generation for being 'weak', or a young adult who's still trying to succeed using the gameplan of yesterday.

Our take: Every generation has its own fair share of economic struggles. It is important to understand how we got here, so we know how to act accordingly.

The following chapter tackles some of the thorniest controversial issues millennials and Gen Z face.

My generation had it worse

ORIGINALLY PUBLISHED:
20 SEP 2022

~~~~~~~~

Some boomers say that millennials are soft and entitled. They think that despite the many advantages afforded to them, millennials have little to show.

Similarly, millennials may think their parents had it easy because they could afford the same things back then, with less.

Here's why this phenomena is a missed opportunity for mutual understanding.

Back in the 1980s, Singapore developed at a rapid pace. Property was cheap.

You could comfortably raise a family with just one parent working.

Hey you - it's easy to think your parents had it easy because they are financially stable today...

But what you don't realize is that they did live through some very uncertain times.

So yes, your parents' homes were far more affordable - even after taking the median salary into account.

However, there was absolutely no guarantee that Singapore's land would be as valuable as it is today.

In an alternate universe, it's entirely possible that Singapore failed to prosper, and turned to other countries for a merger.

That is the risk that your parents took staying here, instead of going somewhere else.

And it paid off.

Finally, you talk about investing in the stock market.

It wasn't until recently that the stock market became easier to invest in, because of technology.
It was incredibly difficult in the past.

Pa, I hungry.

And buying the dip?

Not always easy when you're trying to raise children, or lack the knowledge to do so. If I'm being honest, if you were in his position, you would have done the same.

It is true that technology has made it easier to work and learn... but it has also created a lot of competition.

Unlike you, your son doesn't just compete with other Singaporeans. He competes with the entire world - and there are some really brilliant people out there.

You mock him for not being able to afford a home... but the truth is, wages have not been keeping up with cost of living for quite a while now.

To make matters worse, he will **ALSO** have to go up against automation and AI. Technology is developing at a rapid pace.

In your generation, skills remained relevant for longer. This is no longer the case.

It is the younger generation's duty to study what previous generations have gone through, not just to learn from their mistakes.

...but also appreciate the work that was put in before.

'I must study politics and war that my sons may have liberty to study mathematics and philosophy.

'My sons ought to study mathematics and philosophy, geography, natural history, naval architecture, navigation, commerce, and agriculture, in order to give their children a right to study painting, poetry, music, architecture, statuary, tapestry, and porcelain.'

– John Adams

Stay woke, salaryman.

Why inequality looks the way it does

ORIGINALLY PUBLISHED:
05 DEC 2022

~~~~~~~~

Author's Note:

We know that the world is unequal. How did it get that way? Who is to blame? We highlight two often-overlooked major forces that have had a part to play. By understanding how we got here, it's easier to chart a course on what to do next.

Why inequality looks the way it does

Disclaimer: In case it needed to be said, we do not trivialize or rationalize the suffering caused by inequality. Rather, this article aims to add context to the inequality you have been observing. We hope you find it useful.

What can explain the inequality in the world today?

Recently, we polled our community and received all sorts of answers.

Some people said it was greedy corporations, broken systems, and corrupt politicians creating systems that were inherently unjust.

Others put the blame on 'mindset', 'grit', and 'education', Or the lack thereof.

All these answers are possibly valid in many scenarios and have received quite a lot of coverage. But today, we'd like to steer your attention toward factors we think are equally worth your attention.

They are: shareholder capitalism, globalization, and technology.

Here's what you should know about them.

Shareholder capitalism

It can be a little hard to imagine this today, but in the past, many businesses didn't work to maximize profit. Instead, they incorporated the interests of the different stakeholders working with them. These included:

- Customers
- Government
- Vendors and suppliers
- Employees
- Broader society
- Shareholders

Sometime in the 1970s, the mindset shifted to prioritizing just the shareholder.

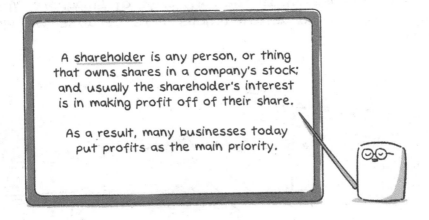

A <u>shareholder</u> is any person, or thing that owns shares in a company's stock; and usually the shareholder's interest is in making profit off of their share.

As a result, many businesses today put profits as the main priority.

Two things happened as a result that would set in motion the wheels of inequality as developed nations know it today.

CEOs had their performances tied heavily to share price, which meant short-term profitability became important. Businesses were no longer looking for win-win scenarios with their stakeholders. They aimed to win at all costs. If you want to read up more about this, check out Jack Welch and the story of General Electric, as well as Milton Friedman.

In turn, businesses looked to cut costs to increase profitability, including manpower costs. How did they do so? After all, shareholder capitalism is only an idea, useless with action.

To get the answer, we need to look at two enablers that allowed shareholder capitalism to prosper: **globalization and technology.**

Globalization giveth, taketh away jobs

A short history lesson: In the early days of Singapore, MNCs brought their manufacturing jobs here because we were cheaper.

We have jobs!

Many of our parents raised us on these jobs, sent us to school, bought homes and contributed to the GDP. All in all, lots of Singaporean boomers have seen a meteoric change in fortunes over the past 50 years.

But where did these jobs come from? Europe and the US.

That's right. When US politicians beat their chest about the 'hollowing out of the middle class', I think it is important to realize that Singaporeans had a part to play in it.

Of course, Singapore is hardly the only culprit – Japan was probably a forerunner.

Taiwan, Hong Kong, and South Korea are likely contemporaries. And in recent years, China. The documentary *American Factory* is particularly poignant.

What is also worth mentioning is that in some ways, the world has become more equal to what it was 50 years ago.

The popular narrative about inequality is that the 1% has prospered at the expense of the middle class. **Inequality within countries has increased.**

Yet at the same time, the last 50 years have seen many poor countries claw their way out of extreme poverty. Singapore, Taiwan, and South Korea were the first wave. But many others have since followed. **Inequality among countries has actually decreased over the last two decades.**

So should we feel guilty about 'stealing' American jobs? In our opinion, these jobs were not 'stolen'.

Business owners made the conscious decision to bring jobs overseas after weighing the pros and cons. Consumers got cheaper products, due to cheaper labour. The only losers? The people who lost their jobs.

But here's the kicker.

Globalization is a double-edged sword.

In the same way that American jobs flowed outwards in the 20th century, Singaporean jobs can also flow out to other countries where labour is more affordable.

Live by the sword, die by the sword, no?

Globalization makes it harder to 'eat the rich'

'Tax the rich!' is the war cry of the disenfranchised. Many of us believe, mistakenly, that governments are able to tax their richest citizens to spend on the poorest.

In reality, the mobility of the rich makes it challenging for governments to play Robin Hood. Two words. Capital flight. Even seemingly all-powerful governments such as the Chinese Communist Party struggle to do so.

Consider this scenario:

Assuming all other things equal, would you choose to pay 17% tax to Singapore, or 40% tax elsewhere?

Most people would pick 17%. And if you were a multimillionaire, you'd probably have the resources to follow through with it.

As the world becomes more connected, assets and money can also easily flow out of a country. This isn't good news for governments, which need tax dollars to fund welfare and education programmes, amongst other things.

Because of globalization, they are forced to compete with each other to attract wealthy citizens and corporations.

This leads to a Catch-22 situation: to get the funds needed to reduce inequality, you have to tax the rich.

...But if you make the country too inhospitable to them, they'd leave for other countries, which will leave the remaining population poorer for it.

There are two implications here:

1. This means that governments increasingly need to deliver value to the wealthy who are paying more taxes. Value in the form of safety, infrastructure, education for children, and most importantly, protection of their interests.

2. Instead of taxing a moderate number of the wealthy heavily, governments will seek to need to tax a large number of the wealthy moderately.

That said, bringing in a large number of wealthy folks into your country quickly also has its ramifications. This brings us to...

Globalization, immigration, and gentrification

Not too long time ago, Tiong Bahru was one of the most affordable neighbourhoods in Singapore. Its buildings were old-fashioned. The shops there catered to its inhabitants - mainly elderly folk.

That changed sometime in the 2010s. Tiong Bahru was 'rediscovered' by hipsters and became desirable. Hipster cafes and trendy restaurants set up shop. Parking lots became harder to find; taken up by BMWs and other continental cars.

And before long, Tiong Bahru became unaffordable to its more senior inhabitants.

This process is known as gentrification. It happens worldwide; other famous examples include SoHo (America), Brunswick (Australia), and Tower Hamlets (UK).

But it also happens to cities and countries on a larger scale.

Imagine this:

Let's say you earn $4,500 a month in Singapore.

Suddenly, multimillionaires arrive in droves in your city. Expats earning $30,000 a month start pushing up rental prices. Some of them are competing with you for dream jobs. They drive cars you can never dream of affording.

All of a sudden, you're priced out of your favourite neighbourhood. Your favourite brunch place prices eggs benedicts at a whopping $48 - and gets away with it!

Even if you get a $500 increment, you'd certainly still feel poorer. And you'd feel resentful.

<u>Technology exacerbates the problems caused by globalization</u>

Finally, exponential technological leaps have magnified many of the issues mentioned above. They make both wins and losses larger, further widening the gap.

The internet has made it even easier for cheaper labour in developing countries to compete. The classic example: Employers can hire a graphic designer in the Phillipines via Fiverr or UpWork. They'll be more affordable than a Singaporean, European, Japanese, or American.

Software and automation have replaced numerous jobs, or at least depressed wage growth. My mom's job as a bookkeeper in the 1990s and 2000s saw her being paid $2,500 a month. Today, 20 years later, $2,500 is still the median benchmark for the role.

Meanwhile, those who wield technology can use it to scale their efforts to achieve high incomes and profits. Tech allows companies like Google to be run with extremely lean teams, compared to traditional staffing numbers. But this means there are fewer jobs available. Same with factories and assembly lines. Or solopreneurs using software to reduce labour costs.

Here's a popular thought: Technology is supposed to make our lives easier, allowing us to do things more quickly and efficiently. It indeed has, for quite a large proportion of society.

However, an equally large proportion of society has had their livelihoods disrupted.

What to do with this information?

Inequality is without a doubt, one of the hottest topics of our generation.

Many conversations about it are emotionally charged and tend to make caricatures of people at both extremes of the wealth spectrum:

The poor are lazy, good-for-nothing bums.

The rich are greedy sociopathic hoarders.

The uncomfortable truth is that the world is a lot more complex. And it's likely that by merely existing in the developed world, you have contributed to inequality, in some way and form.

Here's our take: if you want to make the world a more equal place, you have to do several things first.

Firstly, to avoid a wild goose chase, you have to understand what causes it. This will give your actions some direction.

Secondly, difficult things are seldom done alone. One individual is not enough. Many hands make light work. You'll need to recruit people to work on your causes.

Finally, the people who can change things for the better are often those who have either wealth or talent. Ironically, you might need to amass both to create a more equal world on your own terms.

Is it possible to succeed? Maybe.

But you might also live long enough to become the villain.

Stay woke, salaryman.

How I feel about foreigners moving into my homeland

ORIGINALLY PUBLISHED:
24 APR 2023

~~~~~~~~~

In many major cities around the world, young people face competition from two types of immigrants – wealth and talent.

The former prices them out. The latter outcompete them in the labour market. Both increase the cost of living.

Here's how we think you should react.

Here's something you might have noticed for awhile now - many governments seem to be inviting rich foreigners into your country.

TOP NEWS

Singapore must stay open to foreign talent

Hong Kong offers new visa to woo talent amid brain drain

Thailand joins race to lure foreigners in path to economic boom

We're writing this from Singapore. But if you're in Hong Kong, Bangkok, or Sydney, you might be noticing the same thing.

There are generally two kinds of rich people they're looking for - 'wealth' and 'talent'.

'**Wealth**': High-net-worth individuals. Think multimillionaires and billionaires.

'**Talent**': These are immigrants with special skills that allow them to command high incomes.

Let's get this out of the way first:
this isn't always a good feeling.

Some of the new arrivals people aren't exactly nice. There are the rude, arrogant ones who don't respect the local culture and regulations.

I deeply dislike that.

In addition, an influx of rich foreigners can also drive up prices of certain items.

For example: if your local cafe can sell plates of eggs Benedict at $48 to rich foreigners, why would they sell it to you for less?

This also applies to other things: rent, real estate, taxis, services, etc.

Rationale 1: Wealthy immigrants spend more money

When this happens, businesses get to earn more money.

This creates higher-earning locals, who will spend more money, in turn creating more money for others.

In theory, everyone in the country becomes richer together.

Rationale 2: They can improve our workforce

By working with locals, skilled foreign workers can pass on their skills to them. This will, in turn, allow locals to be globally competitive.

Foreigners who set up businesses here can also create jobs for locals as well.

They do this by:

1) Directly hiring locals.
2) Working with smaller local businesses, which also provide jobs for locals.

Rationale 3: Governments need more taxes to pay for stuff

Many developed countries are facing increasing public costs because of aging populations.

At the same time, their working population has also shrunk.

This means they can collect less tax. Big yikes.

Ideally, this is what governments hope* will happen by attracting wealth and capital:

More productive people in the workforce + rich people spending more money

more tax collected

the more $$$ for government spending.

*But it doesn't always play out this way

Rationale 4: Your country will be worse off

At first glance, a country without these rich newcomers sounds promising.

You think:

Surely, things will be more affordable, life will be more equal.

There will be less competition for good jobs.

LOCAL ONLY

Unfortunately, this is unlikely.

If your government cannot collect enough taxes, then they won't have enough to invest in their country.

This can mean bad or non-existent public services; healthcare, education, police, utilities, etc.

The government might even consider taxing younger folks even more to make up for the shortfall.

In fact, if this goes on for long enough, YOU might even consider leaving for somewhere else that you think is a better deal for you.

When local wealth and talent leaves a country, it's called **capital flight** and **brain drain**, respectively.

The impact on the people who have no choice but to remain in the country?

Fewer jobs. Or even unemployment. A loss of purchasing power.

In the 21st century, countries will be competing vigorously for both **wealth and talent.** The battle has already begun.

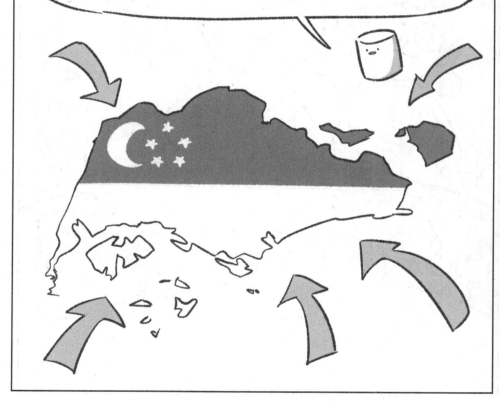

How do you feel as a local on home turf?

Probably poorer. Priced out. Outcompeted.

Let us say this: your feelings are very valid.

Globalization has been kind to some, but
it has been harsh on others as well.

But here's two perspectives worth considering:

Firstly, if your city is doing something that attracts both wealth and talent, this means it is already a fairly good place to live in.

It probably already provides relatively good jobs, opportunities, public services, infrastructure, and safety.

Why?

Think about it: if you were rich and talented, would you choose a lousy place to live in? Probably not.

You'd pick the best option available to you.

Secondly, by being **where** wealth and talent choose to reside, you stand a far better chance of becoming wealthy or talented yourself.

This is compared to places where wealth and talent won't even go near.

Our take? We think it's important to focus on what we can control.

No, you can cannot stop where others choose to come and go.

But you can gain skills and build wealth.

Both will give you options to go where you deem the grass is greener.

It's a big world out there.

Good luck, and all the best.

Stay woke, salaryman.

BE WEALTHIER
THAN THE RICH

The greatest wealth is
to live content with little.

– Plato

CHAPTER 4
BE WEALTHIER THAN THE RICH

Let's assume you've done everything the previous chapters in the book have suggested.

You gained skills that allowed you to earn a good income. You saved. Then you invested. You might even reach financial freedom early, in your 30s or 40s.

Unfortunately, you might still have a poor quality of life.

So far, most of what we've tackled in this book is about how you can amass money and assets. This is extremely important, particularly so if you live in any major city in the world.

However, it's a mistake to think that material riches are the ONLY thing standing between you and a good life.

Here's why.

Why some rich people will never be happy

ORIGINALLY PUBLISHED:
06 MAR 2023

~~~~~~~

Author's Note:

.

Many rich people might have a substantial amount of money. Yet they are still a long way away from happiness. Why? We explore how comparison truly is, the thief of joy.

The one big reason why some rich people will never be happy

Here's a quick diagnosis:

1. Do you have access to food, water, and shelter?

2. Are you relatively healthy with no major sickness?

3. Do you have people that love and care for you?

4. Are you still unhappy?

Yes, yes, yes, yes...

If you answered 'yes' to most of these and live in developed country, there's a high chance you are suffering from

RELATIVE DEPRIVATION

It's a kind of unhappiness that even rich people have.

What is relative deprivation?

It's a form of unhappiness caused by the comparison between one person's situation and another's situation.

When people experience relative deprivation, they feel that they deserve to have or receive the same as others.

Absolute deprivation has clear markers.
It is not dependent on comparison.

For example: Someone who's starving
suffers from absolute deprivation.

So does someone only has 3 hours a sleep a day.

Or someone earning less than what's specified
based on the **national poverty line***.

*Singapore doesn't have an official poverty line, another story for another time.

Over the course of human history, we have created technology so that we've solved many problems of food, water, and safety.

This helps with **absolute deprivation.**

If you're reading this on a smartphone and are not worried about your day-to-day survival, it is likely you do not suffer from absolute deprivation.

thewokesalaryman

Instead, with all the advancements our species have made, we've yet to create technology that helps us overcome relative deprivation.

In fact, with things like social media and globalization, we've might have dug a deeper hole for ourselves.

Think about it: In the past, people could only compare themselves with a smaller circle.

But these days, our basis for comparison has expanded. Greatly.

For example: you might be feeling unhappy because you see other people on social media with nicer, bigger, and newer things than you.

You might also admire someone else with a lot more money than you.

Or celebrities elsewhere you've never met.

Even if you were a multimillionaire, it will still be possible for you to be unhappy - especially if compare yourself with billionaires!
But Dad! My friend Richard just got a rocket!

Look, we're not saying your unhappiness created by relative deprivation is invalid.

It is normal to experience relative deprivation.

However, what is also true is that it hampers your ability to be happy.

If the goal is to be happy, then it's worth exploring how to overcome it.

So, how can we overcome
relative deprivation?

Our research leads us to
believe it's two things:

CONTENTMENT

&

GRATITUDE

CONTENTMENT

Many ancient philosophers suggest that happiness comes from within; not from external factors like being richer, smarter, or better looking than other people.

The old adage is true;
comparison is often the thief of joy.

Aristotle (384 BC to 322 BC) believed that contentment came from acting in accordance with nature and realizing one's full potential. Happiness is self-contentedness.

Buddha encouraged people to seek inner peace, which then leads to contentment and happiness.

GRATEFULNESS

Gratefulness is consistently
linked with greater happiness.

It can help you feel more positive
emotions, relish good experiences,
improve health, and deal with adversity.

Here is a non-exhaustive list of ways to cultivate gratefulness:

♥· Give thanks verbally.

♥· Write thank-you notes.

♥· Keep a gratitude journal.

♥· Focus on the good things that have come into your life, especially small things that you've taken for granted.

All that being said, what is often preventing us from having gratitude is the lack of **perspective**.

So here's something for us to consider: Humanity has lived through famine, war, catastrophic disasters and disease.

Bring out yer dead!

You - reading this - probably have a better standard of living compared to the vast majority of humans who have ever lived.

At least we have food and some warmth!

People didn't need fast cars, huge houses, luxury bags, instaworthy travel pictures to be happy.

This means there is someone out there in the past, who'd be extremely grateful for all that you have today.

People have been happier, with far less.

Like it or not, here's the uncomfortable truth:
happiness might be well within our grasp.

The real question is:
why aren't we choosing it?

Content makes poor men rich;
discontent makes rich men poor.

– Benjamin Franklin

Stay woke, salaryman.

Why I'm shamelessly downgrading

ORIGINALLY PUBLISHED:
25 OCT 2019

~~~~~~

Author's Note:

We live in a society that's consumed by over-consumerism. But what happens when we expect retail therapy and endless upgrading to give us a better life? Here's the case for going against the flow.

Society tells us that bigger and newer is always better.

And the more income we have, the more we MUST spend.

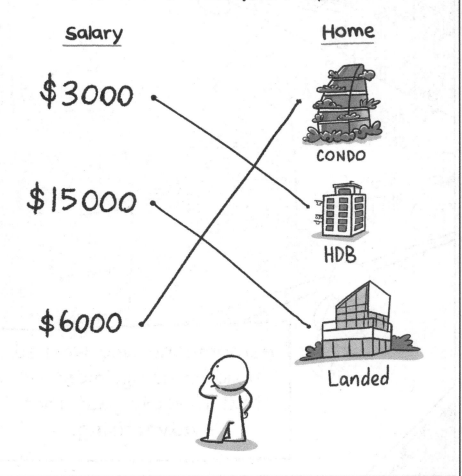

Salary   Home

$3000   CONDO

$15000   HDB

$6000   Landed

Upgrading might make you look good and even feel good, but most things are only <u>temporary</u>.

It's really simple: paying 100% more for something doesn't mean you'll be 100% happier.

That's because there will always be newer, shinier things.

You will buy these things, get sick of them, and then look for newer, shinier things.

It never ends.

Until your money runs out.

Instead of thinking about buying things that I think would make me happy, I've chosen to buy things I can afford, and be happy with that instead.

Of course, being happy with less also has some other very real benefits:

1 Your savings can last you a lot longer if you decide to retire, because you don't spend a lot.

② You'll be more environmentally friendly, because you will consume less as a person.

So if you're worried about not having enough money today, the first thing you should do is to see where you can downgrade.

Here are some examples:

Downgrade your housing

Choosing to spend less on housing can have very real benefits. Use the freed-up cash to pay off your loans, or invest for the future.

Okay, that's a bit too small.

If you're considering retirement, there's no shame moving somewhere more affordable rather than staying in an expensive city.

Instead of struggling to make ends meet, your quality of life might actually improve!

There's a popular saying:

Money may not buy happiness, but I'd rather cry in a Jaguar than on a bus.

– Francoise Sagan

Stay woke, salaryman.

Should I hustle?
Or should I lie flat?

ORIGINALLY PUBLISHED:
25 NOV 2022

~~~~~~~

Some people choose to hustle for a better life. Others decide to reject the conventional ideas of success by 'lying flat'.

Which should you choose and what are the risks of either?

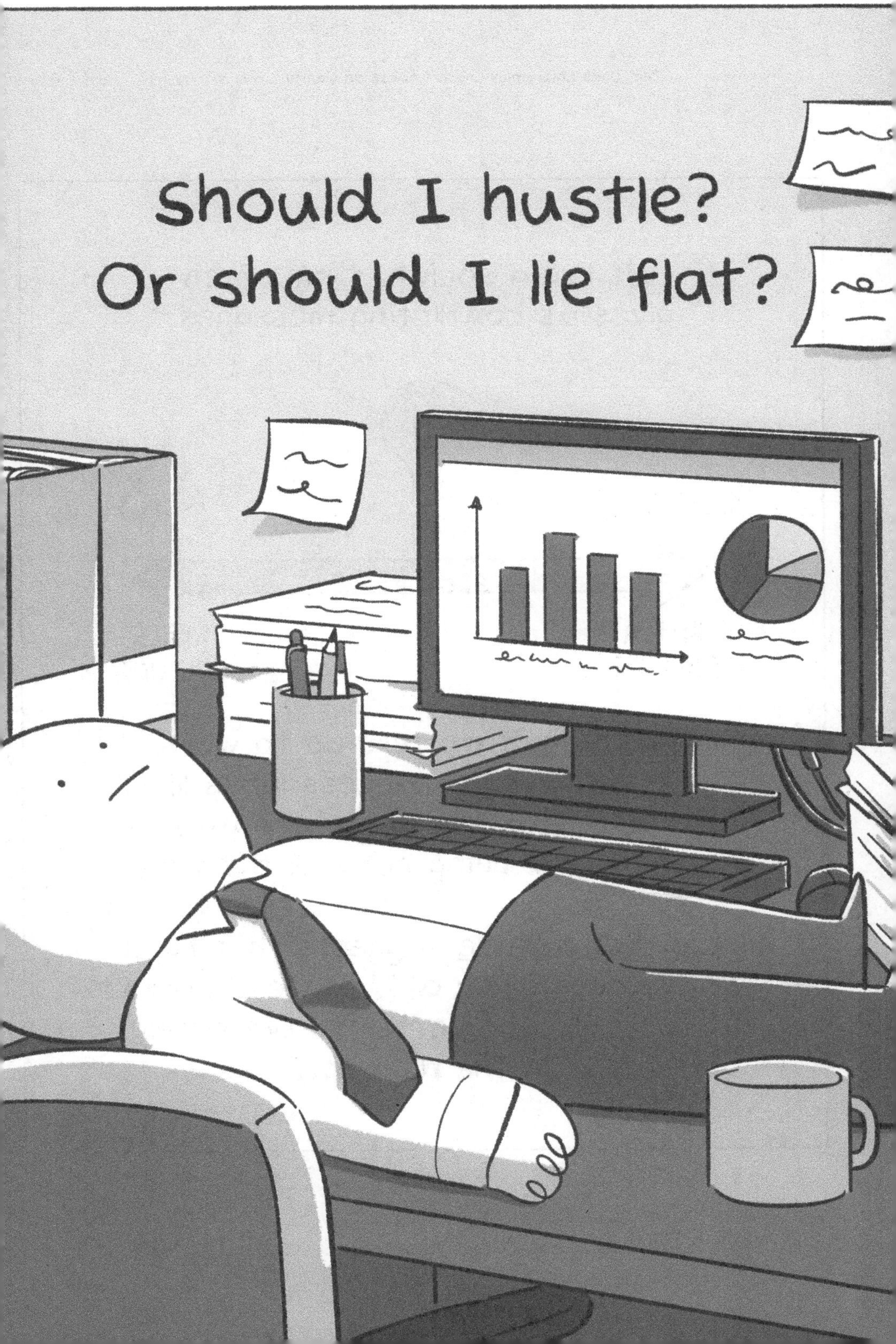
Should I hustle?
Or should I lie flat?

We live a society that often gives us conflicting messages.

LIE-FLAT
CULTURE

HUSTLE
CULTURE

Hustle culture tells us to work our butts off. Success looks like entrepreneurship, large amounts of money, and being busy all the time.

Lie-flat culture suggests that hard work doesn't pay off, so we shouldn't try at all. It's better to live simply in the moment.

Let's start with why you might want to **hustle, first.**

Despite all the negative news about hustle culture, I think it's good, especially when applied in moderation.

'Hustling' to gain skills, knowledge, experience, and network will all enable you to earn more money, which in turn can give you options.

Of course, taken to the extreme, hustle culture becomes toxic, silly, and ironically counterproductive.

Some examples:

- Busy-ness as a badge of honour
- Endless chasing of goals and never finding fulfilment
- Work for the sake of work
- Sacrificing too much time to earn money
- Not resting, leading to burnout

Not to mention, 'hustle culture' has quite a narrow definition of success - measured mostly by how much money you have.

In reality, there are many ways to be successful.

Raising children

Fighting for a cause

SAVE THE ENVR

Being good at a craft

These are all other ways people can be successful.

How about lying flat?

In my experience, lying flat can also be great.

By rejecting traditional ideas of 'success' - such as money, materialism - one can immediately opt out of the rat race.

This is probably why lying flat and other adjacent ideas like 'antiwork' have gained so much popularity.

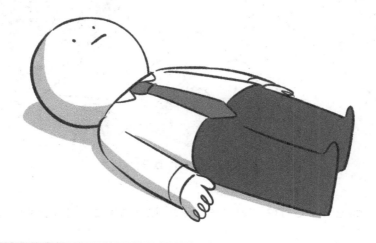

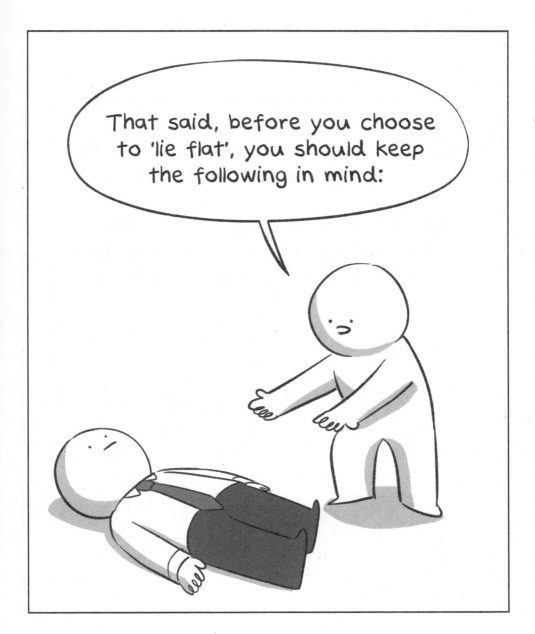

#1 To lie flat is to literally stay still

During this time, others will close the distance, or even overtake you.

Should you decide to get up again in the future, you might realize that you've fallen way too far behind.

#2 Many people want to lie flat, but they don't have goals that are compatible

People often claim they want a simple life, but in reality their lifestyles are neither simple nor affordable.

Spending $3,000 a month, owning a car, living in a popular neighbourhood - this is not the simple life.

#3 Going with the flow isn't always a good idea

Assuming all things remain equal, spending all your salary, paycheck to paycheck sounds like a very attractive idea.

For example: You can get by in your 20s and 30s saving very little. You might think this is sustainable long term.

But here's the thing – life is always changing. People change. The economy changes. Circumstances change. Dreams change.

Without building on your finances, you have limited options to deal with the change.

Lying flat is like going with the flow.
But here's the thing...

People think 'going with the flow' is like this:

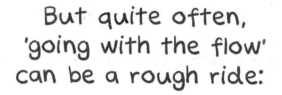

What now?

For the vast majority of people, pursuing extreme ends of the spectrum probably will result in unhappiness.

For me, I choose to be strategic when it comes to **hustling**, and **lying flat.**

For those who hustle, it's important to know your 'enough point' when it comes to money.

The plateau of financial freedom

Lie flat here ——→

The trench of 'more money/ more problems'

The slippery slope of financial hardship

The mountain of money

Hustle here

Faced with a difficult environment,
you have two choices:

Move to another environment.

Or build the capability to lie flat in it.

I've built a boat,
it's not enough for
the Pacific Ocean, but
it should be good
on this lake...

And choices have consequences.

Stay woke, salaryman.

CHAPTER 5

PARTING WORDS

CHAPTER 5
PARTING WORDS

~~~~~~~~

And that's it. Congratulations for reaching the end of our first book!

We've thrown in a couple more comics in the appendix section to describe our general approach to investing.

We're putting it at the end because it can be a bit dry and technical, so treat it as a bonus section to look at when you've paid off your high-interest loans and saved up 6 months of your expenses.

This is just a small first step, but even the most epic journeys begin with a single step.

It won't be easy, but it'll be worth it; we promise.

All the best, and
Stay woke, salaryman.

Thank you for
reading our book.

Appendix

For investing newbs: a simple way to consider financial instruments

Investments can be confusing, with many financial products to look out for in today's complex and highly crowded market.

Here's a concept that can serve as a sense-check when evaluating the different options available in the market.

We call this the magic triangle of investing.

(continued on next page)

THE MAGIC TRIANGLE OF INVESTING

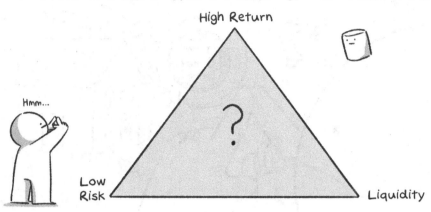

At each end of the triangle lies qualities that all investors will find favourable.

They are:

High return. You can earn a high percentage back on your investment.

Low risk. You're not likely to lose money on this investment.

Liquidity. This investment can be quickly converted into cash without affecting its value.

For better or for worse, you'll be unlikely to get all of these qualities in one investment. You'll at most be able to pick two out of three. Why? Let's take a look.

High returns mean high risk

'Nothing ventured, nothing gained.'

'Fortune favours the bold.'

'If you're not willing to risk the unusual, you gotta settle for the ordinary.'

All these sayings point to one single reality: higher returns *always* come with higher risk.

This is why bonds rated D and are less likely to pay back their debts offer larger yields, and why super safe bonds - such as those rated AAA - tend to offer lower returns.

It is also why conventional financial products typically don't 'guarantee' double-digit returns.

It is far more likely a product guarantees returns of between 1-4% per year. With rising rates, this might go even higher. Yet it is unlikely that few, if any, companies will guarantee a number as high as say, 20% per year.

(Of course, in the defi and crypto space, things are different, but we also know how that turned out.)

High liquidity often means lower returns

Generally, the more quickly you can convert something to cash, the lower the returns, and vice versa. In the investment world, this is known as the liquidity premium.

This 'premium' is an incentive given to people who sacrifice liquidity, hence the name.

Let us explain how it works. Not having liquidity is an undesirable thing. You have money but you can't access it. No one likes that.

So, between locking up money for 5 years and 10 years for the same rate of return, you'd probably opt for the former.

Therefore, to make that 10-year investment more attractive, you'd want to be paid a higher return. An incentive. A reward. And that's why higher liquidity often means lower returns.

Now, let's see how the magic triangle of investing concept holds up in real life.

Instruments that are liquid typically have low risk and low returns

Cash Management Account/Money Market Funds

Hmm...

$

High-Yield Savings Account

$

<u>Cash management accounts/Money market funds:</u>

These are cash accounts where you can put your money in the short term. Usually offered by robo-advisors, new fintech solutions, and brokerages, they're marketed as safer investment options and are highly liquid. You are able to withdraw your money in a matter of days or even hours.

The trade-off? Returns. These tend to have some of the lowest rates of financial products - they might even be lower than the current inflation rate!

High-yield savings accounts

These are bank accounts with accelerated savings rates that reward you for transacting more with them. This includes salary crediting, card usage, and even investments and insurance.

High-yield savings accounts are also marketed as safe and are also highly liquid.

Their returns aren't super high but can be higher than a cash management account - provided you transact enough with the bank.

Instruments that are not liquid have low risk and higher returns

CPF Special Account

Longer-Term Endowment

Government pension accounts

There are many government-administered pension systems around the world that try (not always successfully) to help retirees to at least beat inflation.

Generally, these pension plans will have a higher interest rate than that of money market funds and high-yield savings accounts, but this comes at the expense of liquidity.

Many pension plans have strict withdrawal criteria, most notably age. In Singapore, the CPF Special Account (SA) guarantees 4% per year - a rate that is higher than the historical inflation rate of 2%.

Longer-term endowments

Longer-term endowments are a type of savings plan offered by insurers that have lock-in periods of 10 years or longer. They also offer insurance coverage.

These plans are considered safer and less volatile than assets such as equities, yet they also offer higher returns compared to money market funds and cash management accounts.

Generally, the longer the lock-in period, the higher the return. Generally, long-term endowments return anywhere from 2-5% per year, though a portion of the returns is not always guaranteed.

(As interest rates rise, returns might increase as well. They will generally always offer you higher rates than shorter-term options.)

Instruments that are somewhat liquid have high risk and potentially high returns

Stocks,
Unit Trusts,
& ETFs

Stocks, Unit Trusts, and ETFs

Stocks are tiny pieces of public companies that you can buy online. These include popular names like Apple, Tesla, Google, and Microsoft.

Unit trusts are any type of fund that comprises a portfolio of various investment instruments like stocks and bonds and is managed by a professional. This could be an individual or an organization like an asset management company.

ETFs are similar to unit trusts, but they are traded on the market. Hence the name, exchange-traded fund. Commonly known ETFs: CSPX, IVV, ARKK-ETF, QQQ, STI-ETF, and SPY.

These financial instruments all have the potential to earn higher returns than everything listed here, but they also come with high risk.

There are no guaranteed results here. As they say, past performance is not indicative of future results.

Note: We say these are 'somewhat' liquid, because even though you can sell off these instruments relatively quickly, you might make a loss due to the volatility of these assets.

Finally, some important caveats to note

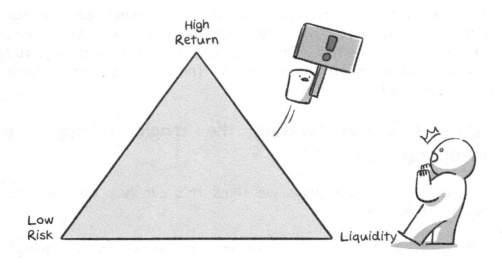

While the triangle is a good way to understand the various investment options you have available to you, there are some things that need to be taken into account.

This triangle serves as a guide, but it is not the rule.

One example: typically, longer-duration bonds have higher yields than shorter-duration bonds because of the liquidity premium mentioned earlier.

However, in times when investors fear recession, this relationship might be reversed. This is known as the inverse yield curve.

Exceptions do happen; there are other mechanisms in play. Risk, return, and liquidity generally apply to all investments. But there are other factors involved too that will affect how the instrument behaves.

For example, to increase returns on a high-yield savings account, you often have to transact more with the bank. 'Transactions' are not related to risk, return, or liquidity, but are instead an incentive created by the bank, as part of their business model.

Why is understanding the magic triangle of investing important?

There are two main ways we think this can help anyone who wants to invest.

The first is to <u>temper optimism</u>. The world has a serious investment scam problem. Last year, Singaporeans lost more than $663 million in scams, much of it to investment scams. Scammers often promise guaranteed high returns within a short span of time.

Understanding the triangle will hopefully help you view such scams with extra caution.

The second point is to appreciate how <u>different investments all have a role</u> to play in your portfolio, and it does not pay to be fixated on 'max returns' as the only goal.

While not as fashionable, liquidity and the safety of your investments are equally, if not sometimes more important.

After all, if there's one thing more awesome than double- or even triple-digit returns, it's actually being able to use your money to lead the life you want.

Stay woke, salaryman.

Building a Globally Diversified Portfolio via ETFs for Beginners

"(Information accurate as of November 2023)"

Introduction

If you're interested in managing your own portfolio but you're not sure where to start, here's a beginner-friendly guide to doing it yourself with a range of ETFs that offer both diversification and affordability.

If you want a one-stop solution: VWRA

Ticker: VWRA (Vanguard FTSE All-World UCITS ETF USD Acc)

This ETF covers the entire global stock market, giving you diversified exposure to companies across the globe. However, remember that it only involves stocks and excludes other asset classes like bonds or real estate.

> *Quick note: If you're content with this information, feel free to stop reading here. However, if you're interested in a more nuanced approach, keep reading.*

Alternatives to VWRA include:

VWRD: Similar to VWRA but distributing dividends, instead of accumulating them. Distributing means that dividends will be transferred to you, the shareholder; accumulating means dividends will automatically be reinvested back into the fund.

VT: Another excellent all-world ETF.

We like VWRA because it reinvests dividends back into the fund, effectively increasing its net asset value. For Singaporean investors, this strategy is beneficial as foreign dividends are taxed at 30%, dampening your overall returns.

U.S. market investments

When people refer to 'the market,' they're talking about the S&P 500 — a stock market index that tracks the 500 largest U.S. companies. For anyone investing in the S&P 500 through Singapore, we think **CSPX** is a solid choice after accounting for taxes and management fees.

S&P 500 tickers: CSPX, SPLG, IVV, VOO, SPY

Tech-focused options: QQQ, and QQQM

The Invesco QQQ ETF tracks the NASDAQ-100 Index, offering investors exposure to 100 of the largest non-financial companies listed on the NASDAQ. Popular for its tech-heavy portfolio, QQQ is considered a growth-oriented investment. It offers diversification across sectors, high liquidity, and a lower expense ratio compared to actively managed funds.

However, it comes with its own set of risks, such as market volatility and concentration in the tech sector.

Chinese market

Regulatory changes have unnerved many investors in recent years. However, we think the long-term growth potential of China as an emerging superpower is still worth considering.

Broad option: MCHI (iShares Core MSCI China ETF)
Tech-focused option: KWEB (KraneShares CSI China Internet ETF)

For the purposes of risk management, we recommend keeping your China market investments within a controlled range, for example 10% of your portfolio.

Your local market

Last but not least, there's also merit in investing in your local stock market, even if the growth prospects are not as high. Why?

Because being familiar with market conditions and industries aids informed decision-making. Local investments eliminate currency risk and often come with tax benefits, improving overall returns. Additionally, lower transaction costs make domestic investing cost-efficient.

You can do this via your local index fund.

Conclusion

Our approach to investing centres on consistent, moderate growth while minimizing risks. Long-term wealth doesn't usually come from miraculous short-term gains. Instead, it's about earning a stable income, smart investing, and frugal living.

To use a gaming analogy: think of your income as the carry and your investments as the support. Together, they protect your net worth against inflation and enable you to meet your investment objectives.

Ultimately, investing in yourself remains the wisest choice. Keep learning, stay invested, and live within your means.

Stay woke, salaryman.

INDEX